COLORING CALENDAR
COOKBOOK
FOR KIDS
A "PERPETUAL"
WRITE-IN CALENDAR
WITH RECIPES
BY AILEEN PAUL
ILLUSTRATIONS BY GARY CHEW

Sunstone books may be purchased for educational, business, or sales promotional use.
For information please write: Special Markets Department, Sunstone Press,
P.O. Box 2321, Santa Fe, New Mexico 87504-2321.
Printed on acid-free paper

ISBN: 978-0-91327-090-5

Dear Boys and Girls~

This is YOUR calendar—a special coloring and cooking calendar
You might want to start by filling in the dates for each of the months.
An already printed calendar is a good guide and you can ask a grown-up for help if you need to.

We think you can use the Coloring Calendar Cookbook in many ways:

Begin cooking with the recipe of the month or…
If you want to cook, but the time is not right, color the pictures and cook later.
If you do not like to cook (and that would surprise me), use this book as a calendar only.

The important thing is to remember: it is your calendar. Have fun with it!

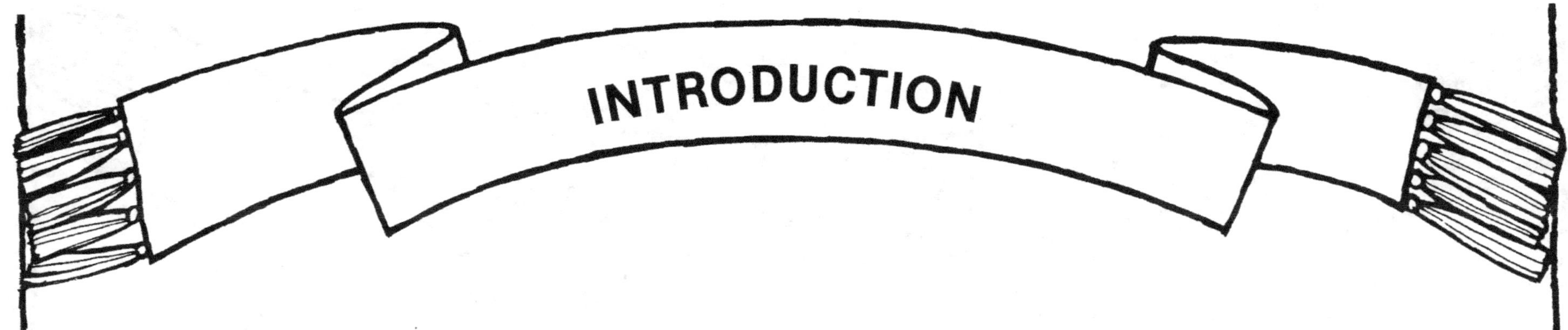

COOKING TERMS

BAKE	To cook in the oven.
BEAT	To mix with quick stirring motion.
BLEND	To combine two or more ingredients until they are smooth and look like one.
BOIL	To heat liquid until bubbles form.
CHOP	To cut in little pieces.
GRATE	To rub food through a grater which cuts the food into various sizes.
MIX	To combine ingredients by stirring.
PREHEAT	To turn on or light an appliance and heat to a certain temperature before putting food in to cook.
SIMMER	To cook slowly over low heat with bubbles forming and breaking *below* surface.

COOKING STEPS

1. Read recipe carefully before you start.
2. Be sure you have everything to work with.
3. Place ingredients and equipment together.
4. Keep a garbage pail handy.
5. Put a sponge in a convenient spot.
6. Have paper towels or dish cloth nearby.
7. Wash your hands with soap and water before you begin.

SAFETY RULES

1. Use electric mixer or any electrical equipment *only* with an adult.
2. Use a paring knife for your cutting. Ask for grown-up help if you use a different one.
3. Use a wooden chopping board for cutting.
4. Use dry pot holders at all times.
5. Turn handles of utensils so that they will not be knocked off stove or counter.

GROWN-UPS

Older people can be helpful.
Let a grown-up do the following:

1. Turn on, or light the oven or stove burners.
2. Put food in oven and remove it.
3. Pour hot water or drain hot foods.
4. Ask an adult if you do not understand a word or cooking term.

CANDIED
PECANS
PECANS
JANUARY

HERE'S WHAT YOU NEED:

1½ cups sugar

½ cup water

1 teaspoon orange or vanilla extract

2 cups pecan halves

1½ quart saucepan

mixing spoon

1-cup measuring cup

measuring spoons

candy thermometer

wax paper

cutting board

HERE'S WHAT YOU DO:

1. Measure sugar, water and extract and pour into saucepan. Stir until dissolved.

2. Place over medium heat. Continue to stir now and then until mixture boils. Do not stir once mixture begins to boil.

3. Place candy thermometer in syrup (sugar and water cooked together are syrup.) Cook until thermometer reaches 240°F, or soft ball stage. (Test for soft ball stage is to drop about ½ teaspoon of syrup into cold water. If it sticks together, that's soft ball stage.)

4. Remove immediately from heat using a pot holder. Place on wooden board.

5. Add nuts and stir gently with spoon until syrup looks cloudy.

6. Tear off a large square of wax paper. Spoon candied pecans onto paper. Separate with fork, if necessary, and cool.

Makes about 36 pieces.

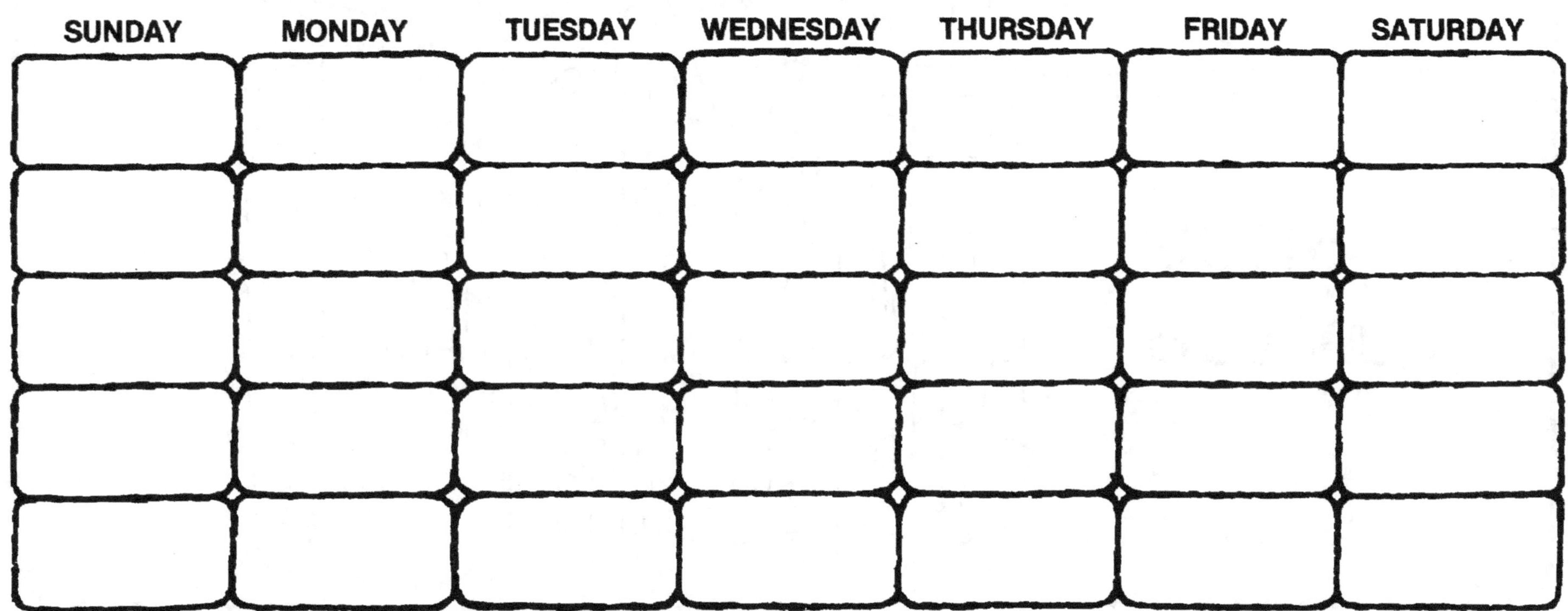

POTATO
SOUP
FEBRUARY

HERE'S WHAT YOU NEED:

- 2 large potatoes
- 2 large onions
- 8 slices bacon or ¼ pound salt pork
- 1 can (1 pound) tomatoes
- 1 teaspoon salt
- ⅛ teaspoon pepper
- vegetable peeler
- paring knife
- cutting board
- large saucepan
- fry pan
- slotted spoon

HERE'S WHAT YOU DO:

1. Peel potatoes and onions. Cut into small pieces with paring knife on board.

2. Put in large saucepan and cover with water. Place over high heat. Bring to a boil and lower heat to simmer for about 10 minutes.

3. While vegetables are cooking, cut bacon or pork into small pieces. Cook in fry pan over medium heat until golden brown, but not too crisp.

4. Remove bacon or pork with slotted spoon. Add to vegetables along with about a teaspoon of bacon fat.

5. Add can of tomatoes and simmer for 10 minutes.

6. Season with salt and pepper.

   Makes 4 servings.

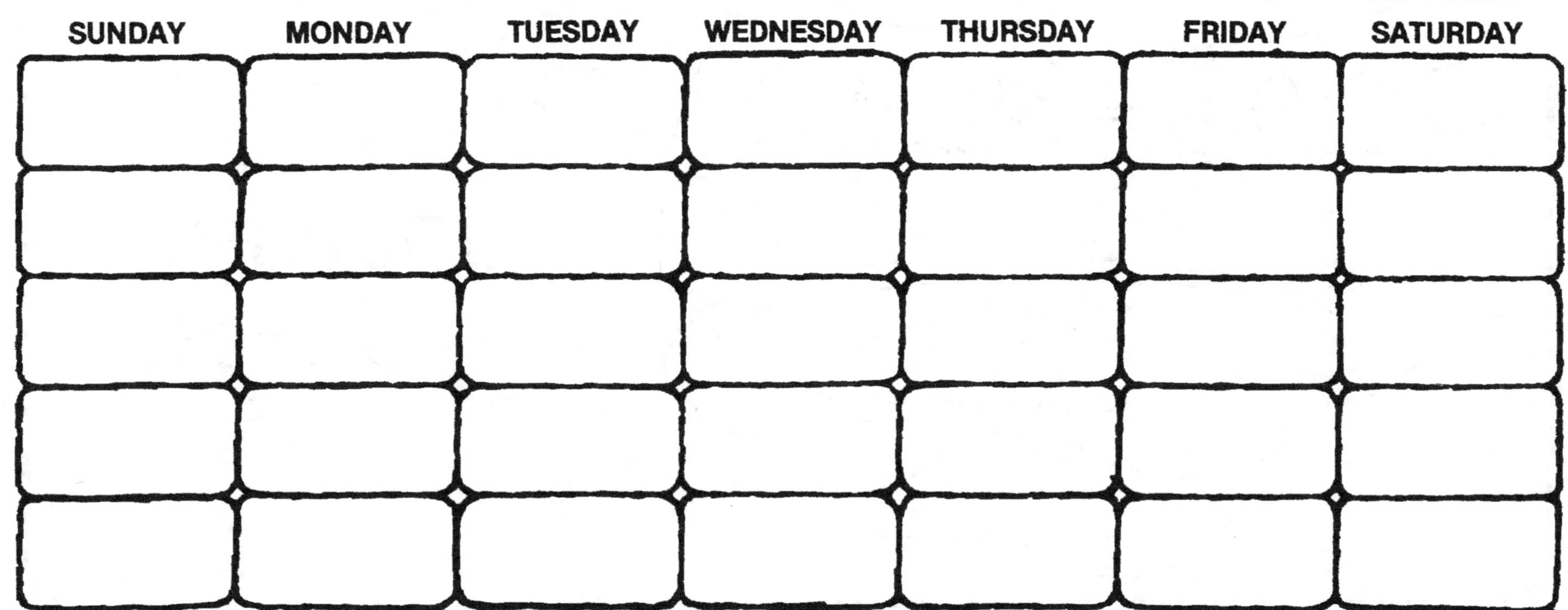

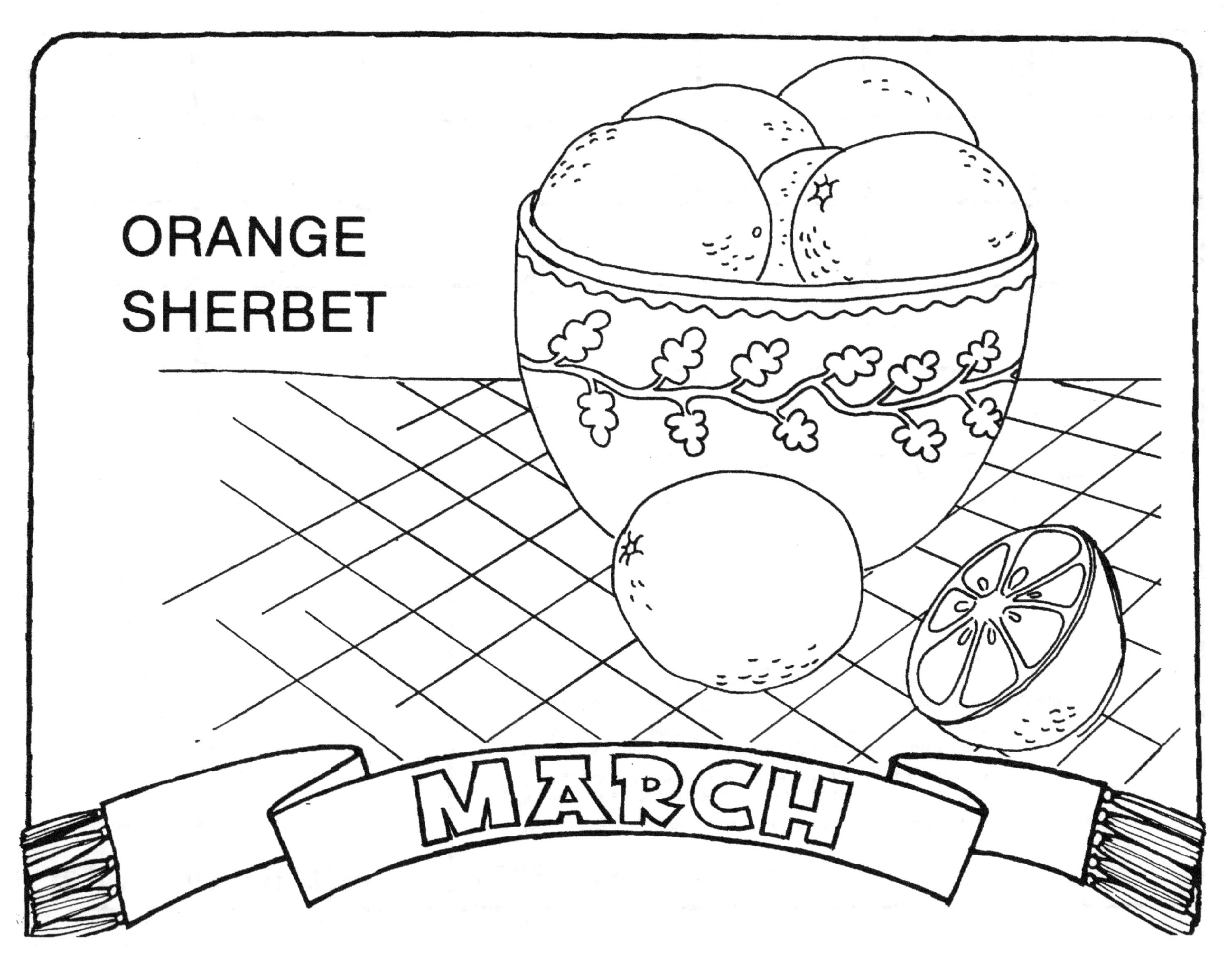

ORANGE
SHERBET
MARCH

HERE'S WHAT YOU NEED:

3 or 4 oranges
1 cup sugar
¾ cup corn syrup
2 cups water
grater
measuring spoons
1-cup measuring cup
medium saucepan
juice squeezer
refrigerator ice trays (without dividers)
mixing bowl
egg beater
cooking spoon

HERE'S WHAT YOU DO:

1. Grate orange rind, enough for 1 tablespoon.
2. Measure and pour sugar, corn syrup, orange rind and 2 cups of water into saucepan. Place over low heat and stir until sugar is melted.
3. Remove from heat and cool syrup.
4. Squeeze 2 cups of orange juice and add to cooled syrup.
5. Pour mixture into refrigerator ice trays. Place in freezer until firm.
6. Place mixing bowl and beaters in refrigerator to chill.
7. Remove frozen mixture from tray to mixing bowl and break up with spoon. Beat with beater until it becomes a thick mush.
8. Spoon back into trays. Return to refrigerator and freeze again.

   Makes 4 to 6 servings.

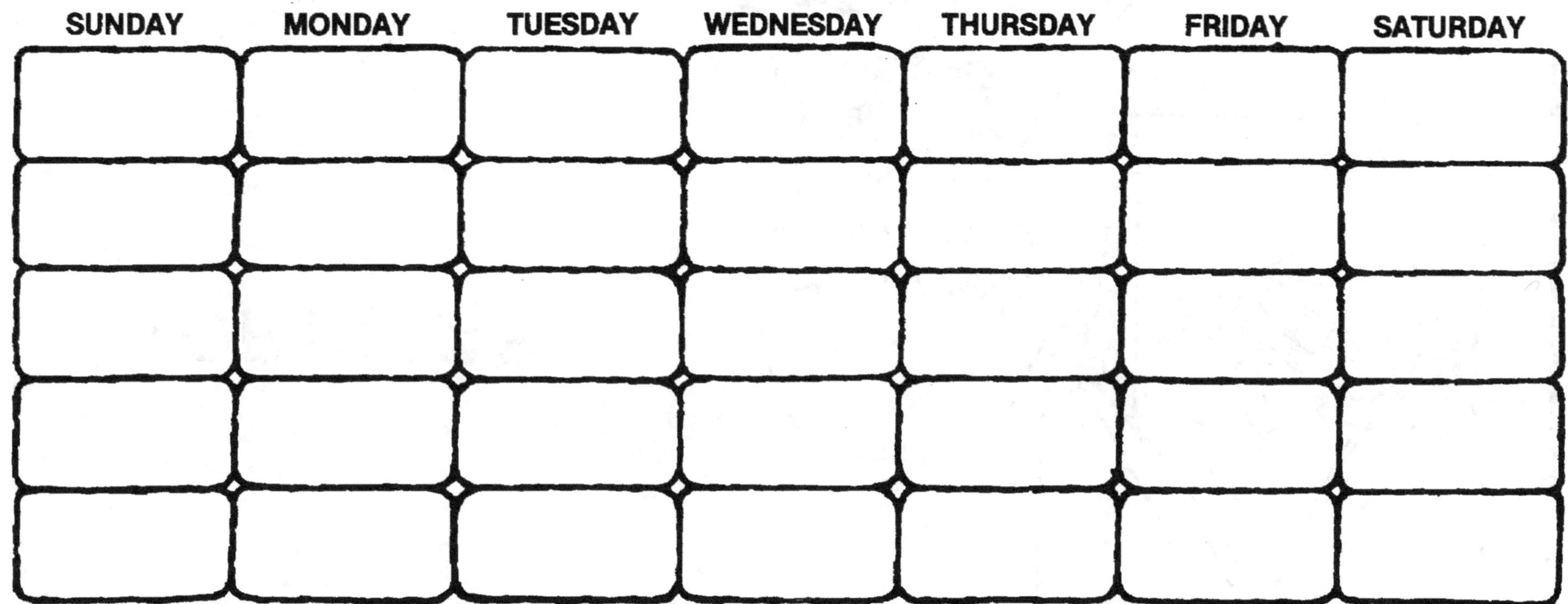

TORTILLAS
APRIL

HERE'S WHAT YOU NEED:

- 4 cups all-purpose flour
- 2 teaspoons salt
- 4 teaspoons baking bowder
- 4 tablespoons shortening at room temperature
- 1½ cups warm water, approximately
- measuring cup
- measuring spoons
- large mixing bowl
- table fork
- pastry blender or 2 table knives
- pancake griddle or heavy fry pan

HERE'S WHAT YOU DO:

1. Measure flour, salt and baking powder into large bowl. Stir gently with fork to mix.

2. Measure and cut softened shortening into flour with a pastry blender or two knives. Continue until mixture is crumbly, almost like coarse sand.

3. Sprinkle warm water, several teaspoons at a time, over flour mixture, and work dough with hands until dough is stiff enough to handle.

4. Knead dough 15 to 20 times. (To knead means to press the dough flat with the palm of your hand; then fold the dough back on itself and push lightly again.) Let dough stand for 10 minutes covered with towel or transparent plastic wrap.

5. Make balls from dough the size of an egg. Roll out in 6-inch circles.

6. Grease griddle with small amount of shortening. Heat griddle to high. Cook each tortilla about two minutes on one side. Turn and cook one minute longer.

Makes 8 to 12 tortillas.

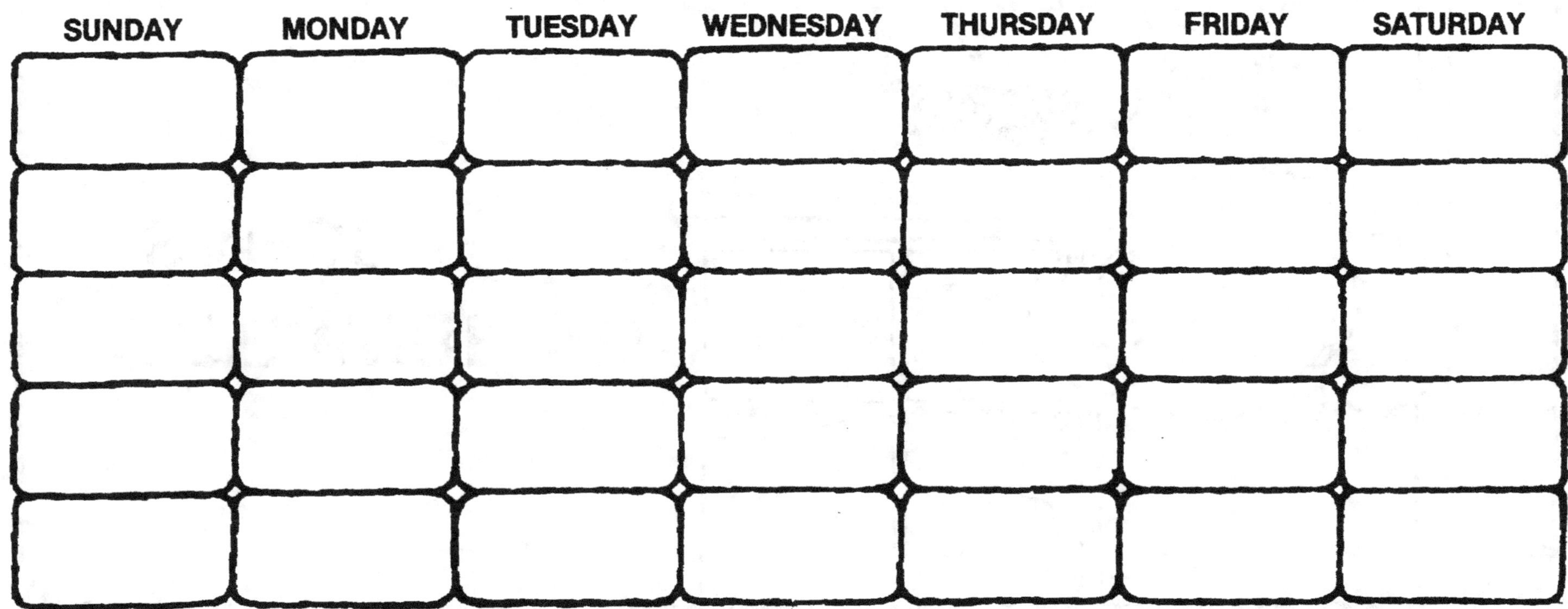

STRAWBERRY
SAUCE
MAY

HERE'S WHAT YOU NEED:

1½ cups fresh ripe strawberries

¼ cup sugar (or less)

1 cup water

2 teaspoons corn starch

¼ cup water

1-cup measuring cup

strainer and/or colander

measuring spoons

mixing spoon

paring knife

cutting board

HERE'S WHAT YOU DO:

1. Remove hulls; wash berries under running water. Do not soak. Drain in colander.

2. Rub ¾ cup berries through strainer with back of spoon. Cut remainder of berries in slices on cutting board with paring knife.

3. Measure sugar and water into saucepan. Stir to dissolve.

4. Measure and dissolve corn starch and ¼ cup water in measuring cup. Add to sugar mixture.

5. Place pan over medium to high heat. Bring mixture to a boil, stirring until sauce thickens and becomes clear. Gently add strawberries.

Serve warm or cold over ice cream, cake or pudding.

Makes about 2 cups.

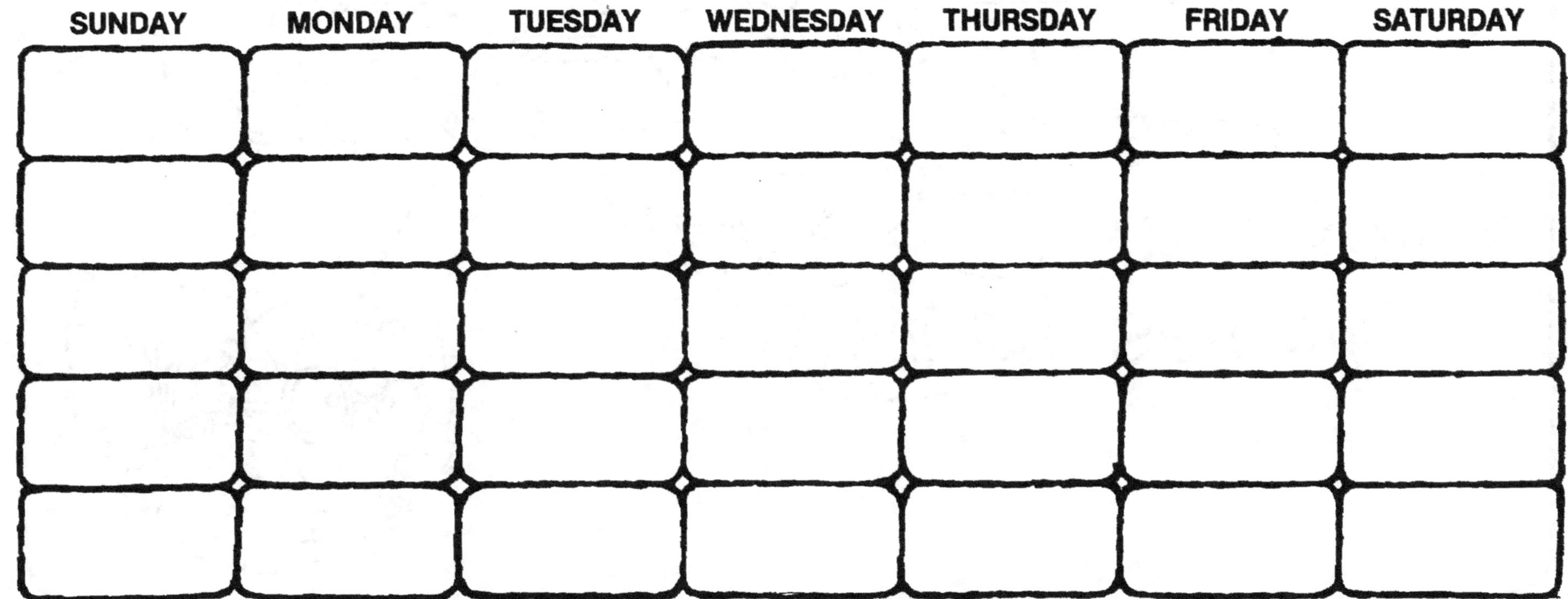

SPICY
CHICK-PEA
SNAK
JUNE

HERE'S WHAT YOU NEED:

1-pound can chick-peas
½ stick butter or margarine
1 teaspoon garlic powder
½ teaspoon dry mustard
½ teaspoon chili powder
1 teaspoon salt
1 teaspoon onion powder
sieve or colander
large fry pan
measuring spoons
mixing spoon
baking pan

HERE'S WHAT YOU DO:

1. Drain chick-peas in colander.
2. Melt butter in large skillet over medium heat.
3. Measure and stir garlic powder, dry mustard, chili powder, salt and onion powder into butter. Lower heat. Stir until thoroughly blended, about 5 minutes.
4. Turn oven on to 350°F.
5. Spoon chick-peas into seasoned butter. Stir lightly until coated.
6. Spread chick-peas on baking pan. Use pot holders and place in oven. Bake about 20 to 30 minutes until chick-peas are crisp, but not too brown. (You may need adult help with oven.)

Makes approximately 2 cups.

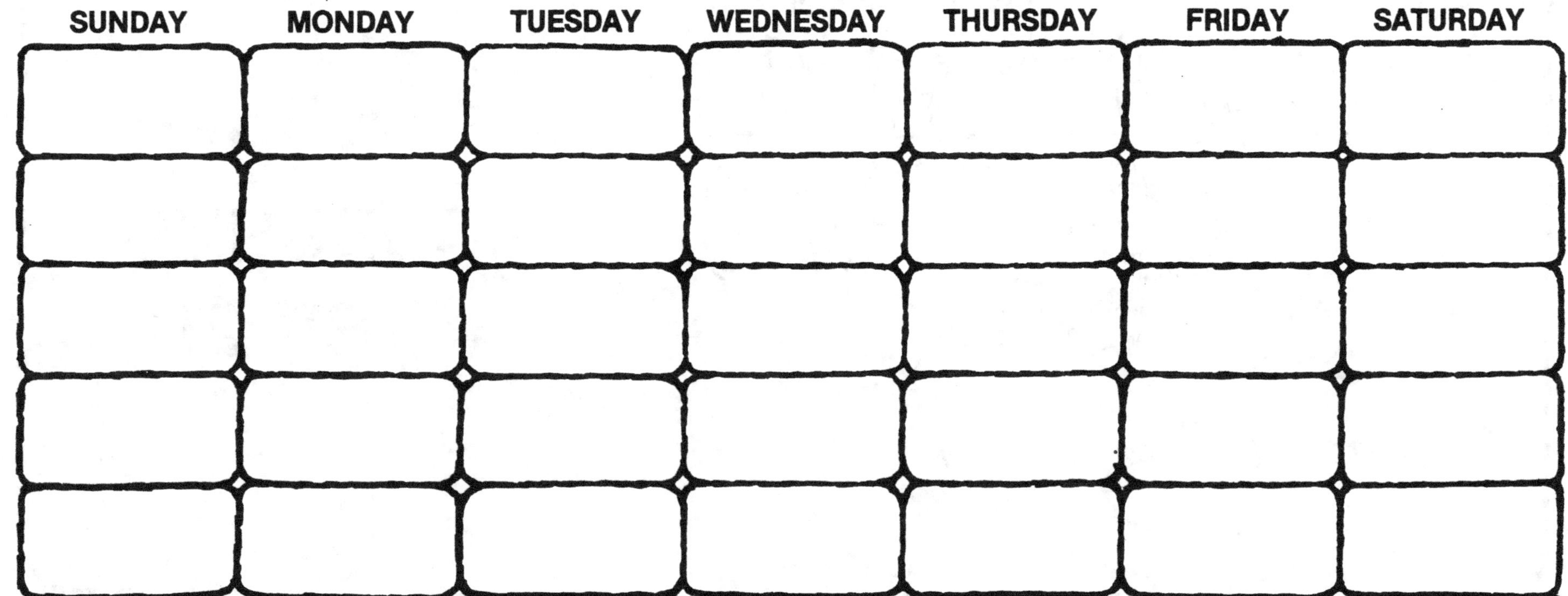

SUNDAY
MONDAY
TUESDAY
WEDNESDAY
THURSDAY
FRIDAY
SATURDAY

TEXAS
BARBECUE
SAUCE
JULY

HERE'S WHAT YOU NEED:

2 cups catsup

⅔ cup Worcestershire sauce

½ cup vinegar

1 teaspoon garlic salt

⅛ teaspoon cayenne pepper

2 tablespoons vegetable oil

1-cup measuring cup

measuring spoons

medium saucepan

mixing spoon

HERE'S WHAT YOU DO:

1. Measure and pour all ingredients into saucepan.

2. Place on medium to high heat and bring to a boil.
   Lower heat immediately and simmer for 20 minutes.

   Serve over hamburgers, frankfurters or other cuts of meat.

   Refrigerate leftover sauce.

   Makes 3½ cups.

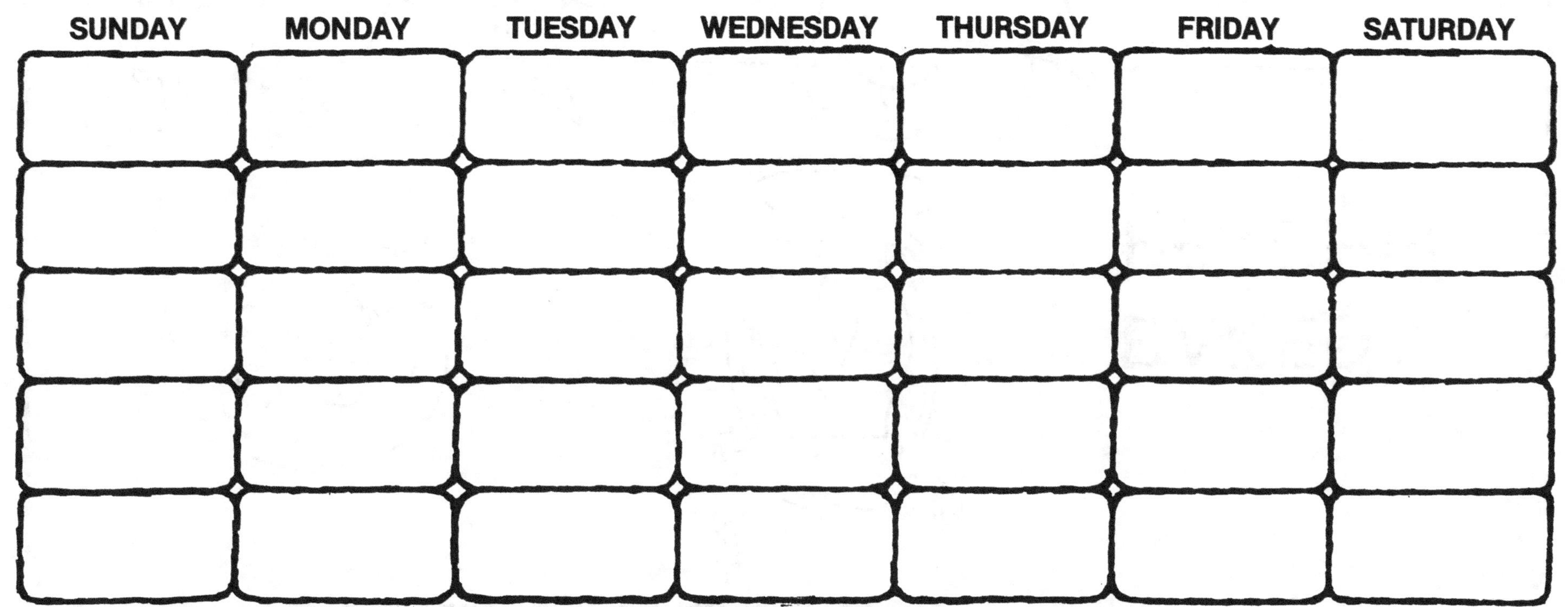

BAKED
PEACHES
AUGUST

HERE'S WHAT YOU NEED:

4 tree-ripened peaches

1 tablespoon lemon juice

8 or 10 macaroons or vanilla wafers

small amount of butter

paring knife

cutting board

small spoon

baking dish

pot holders

HERE'S WHAT YOU DO:

1. Wash and dry peaches. Do not peel.

2. Cut each peach in half with paring knife on cutting board. Remove pit.
   Sprinkle with lemon juice to prevent peach from turning dark.

3. Preheat oven to 350°F.

4. Crumble macaroons and spoon into each peach half. Dot with butter.

5. Place fruit in baking dish and add small amount of water to cover bottom of pan.

6. Use pot holders and put pan in oven on center rack.

7. Bake until tender, 15 to 20 minutes.
   Do not overcook.

   Makes 4 servings.

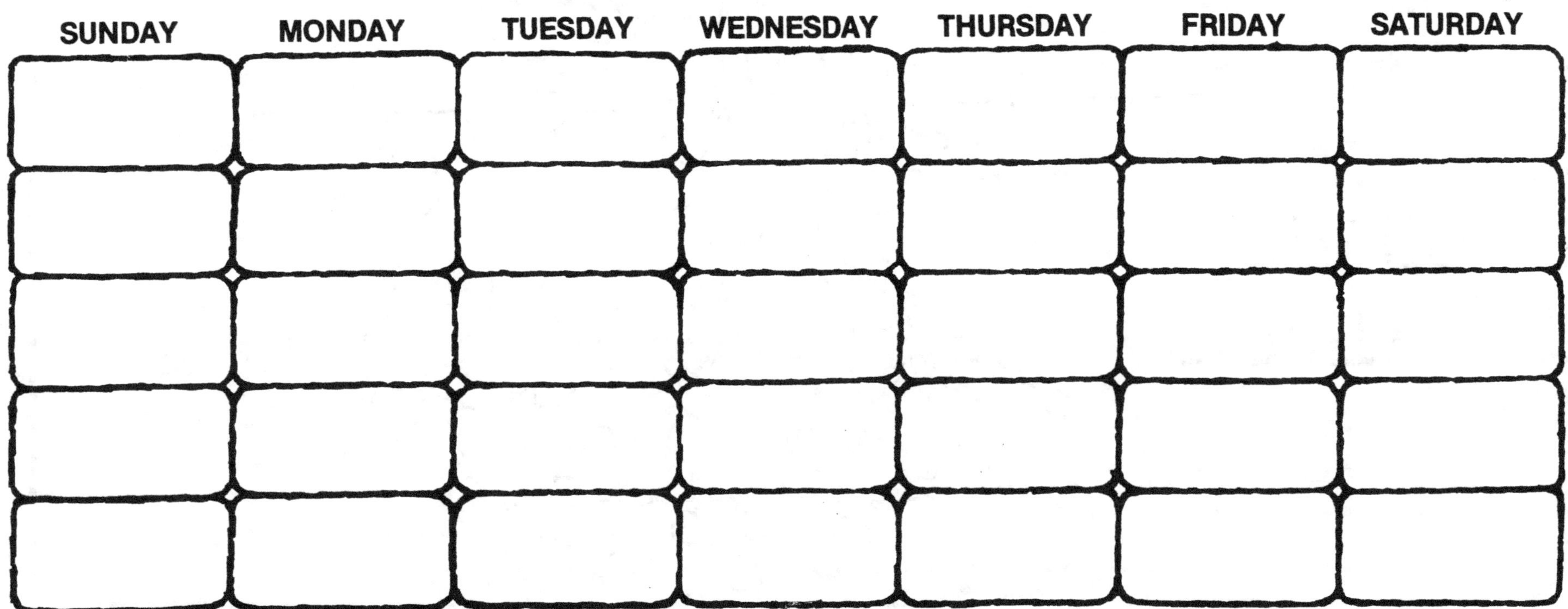

DRIED APPLES
SEPTEMBER

HERE'S WHAT YOU NEED:

Ripe firm apples

3 tablespoons salt

2 quarts water

vegetable peeler

paring knife

large glass bowl

measuring spoons

1-quart measuring utensil

colander

racks or baking tins

HERE'S WHAT YOU DO:

1. Wash, peel and core apples. Cut into thin slices.
2. Measure and add 3 tablespoons salt to 2 quarts water. Drop slices into salted water. Let stand 10 to 15 minutes. Drain.
3. Place apple slices in single layers on drying racks, baking tins or large clean cloth.

FOR SUN DRYING
1. Place on table outside or on porch roof. To protect from dirt and animals, cover with screen or thin clean cloth.
2. Turn occasionally.
3. Bring in each day before sundown to keep fruit from getting wet.
4. Dry in sun 3 to 5 days, depending upon heat and moisture. Fruit is dry when it feels leathery.

FOR OVEN DRYING
1. Preheat oven to 150°F.
2. Place racks or baking tins in oven. Leave space for air to circulate.
3. Leave oven door open slightly to allow moisture to escape.
4. Dry about 12 hours.

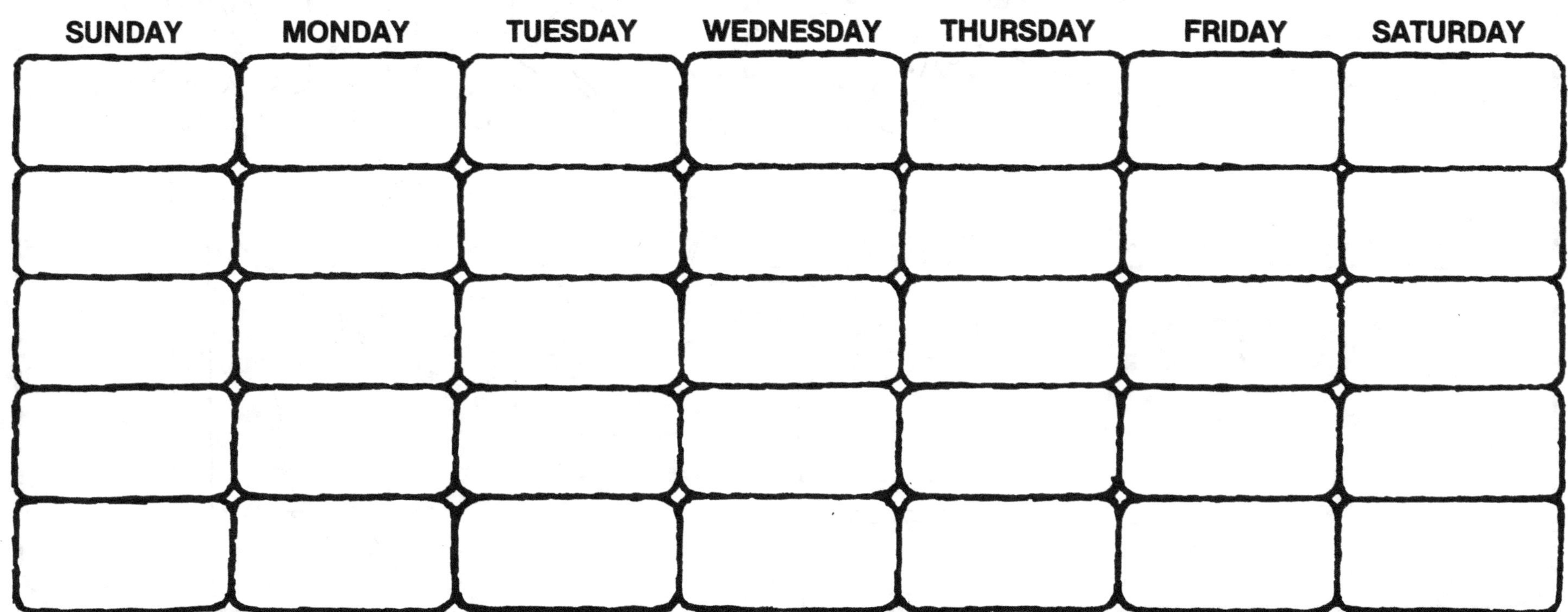

MELON
SUPREME
10
OCTOBER

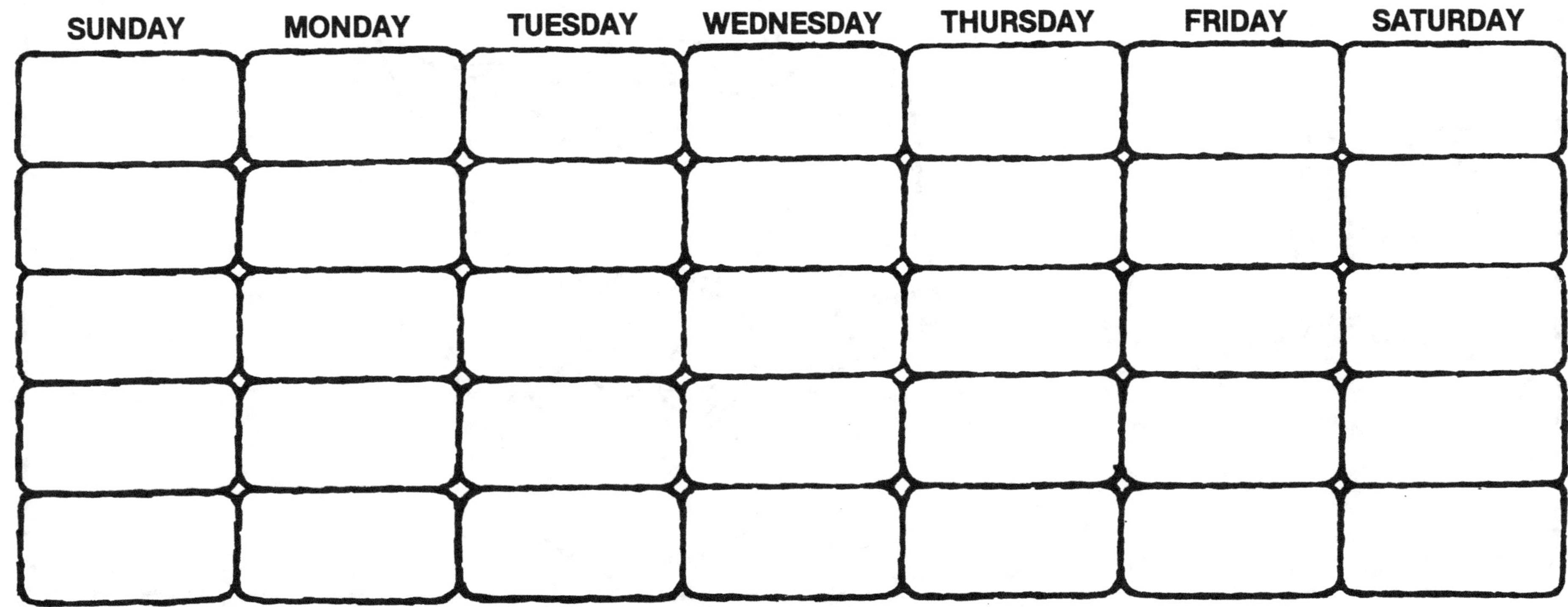

HERE'S WHAT YOU NEED:

- 1 very ripe small honeydew melon
- 1 package unflavored gelatin
- 1⅓ cups unsweetened apple juice
- paring knife
- cutting board
- colander and/or strainer
- mixing spoon
- 1-cup measuring cup
- medium saucepan
- bowl

HERE'S WHAT YOU DO:

1. Slice honeydew in half. (You may need adult help.)

2. Remove seeds and scoop out melon pulp. Press portion of melon through strainer with back of wooden spoon. You need about ½ cup of strained melon. Chop another ½ cup of melon into small pieces.

3. Mix unflavored gelatin with unsweetened apple juice in medium saucepan. Stir over low heat until gelatin dissolves.

4. Pour into bowl and refrigerate until thickened.

5. Remove and stir in melon.

   Chill until firm.

   Makes 4 servings.

BEEF WITH CHILE
BEANS
NOVEMBER

HERE'S WHAT YOU NEED:

1½ pounds beef, round or chuck

1 can (4 ounces) green chilies or

1 teaspoon chile powder

1 1-pound can tomatoes

1 teaspoon garlic powder

1 1-pound can frijoles or kidney beans

1 teaspoon salt

large soup pot

paring knife

measuring spoons

HERE'S WHAT YOU DO:

1. Put beef in large pot; cover with water. Place on high heat and bring to a boil. Lower heat, cover and simmer for about 1 hour.

2. Chop drained chilies and tomatoes with paring knife. Add to beef along with garlic powder. Simmer another hour, or until meat is tender when pierced with fork.

3. Remove meat to plate. Cut into small pieces. Return to pot. (You may need adult help.)

4. Add drained beans and continue cooking until they are heated.

   Season with more salt if needed.

   Makes 4 servings.

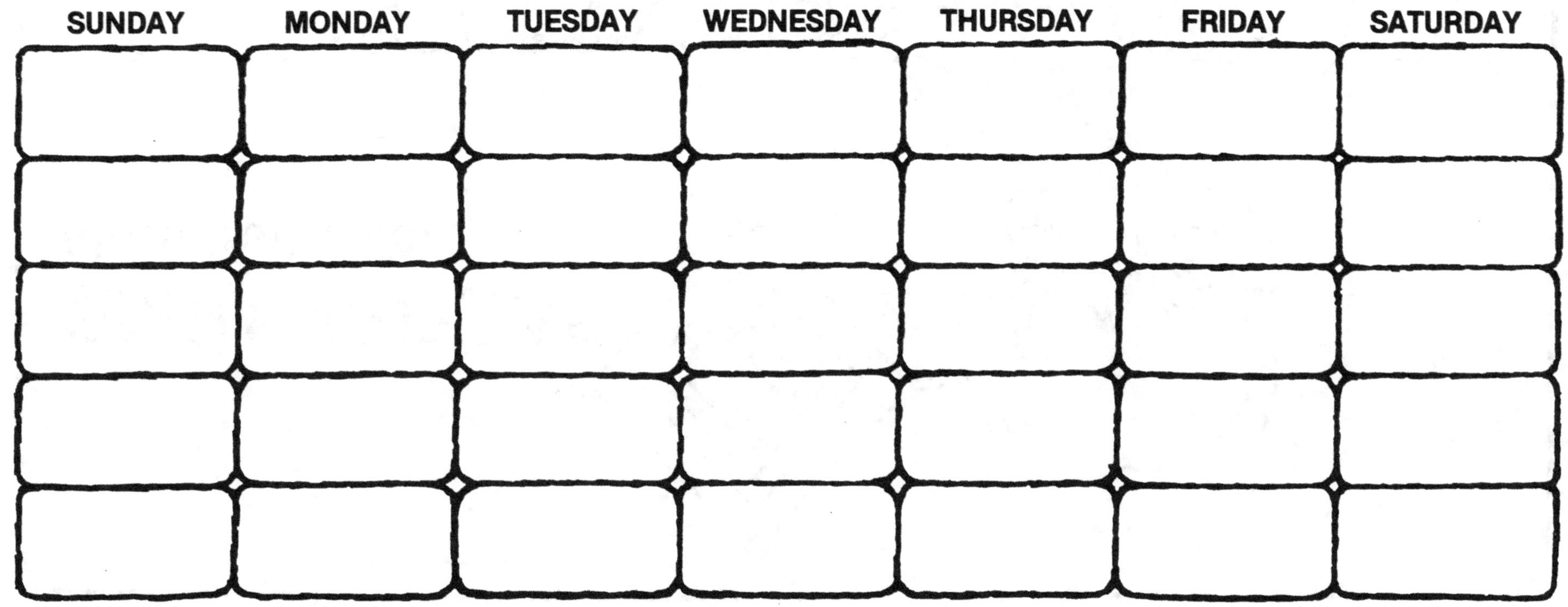

EMPANADITAS
(little fruit pies)
DECEMBER

HERE'S WHAT YOU NEED:

2 cups dried peaches, apricots or apples

½ cup raisins

1 cup sugar, or less

1 teaspoon cinnamon

½ teaspoon nutmeg

¼ teaspoon salt

2 packages prepared pie mix or your own pastry

medium-sized sauce pan

1 cup measuring cup

colander and/or strainer

measuring spoons

mixing spoon

biscuit cutter or wide jar lid

spatula

cookie sheet and cake rack

HERE'S WHAT YOU DO:

1. Bring water to boil in teakettle.
2. Measure fruit and spoon into saucepan. *Let an adult* pour boiling water over fruit, enough to cover. Soak fruit while you prepare pastry.
3. Prepare piecrust following instructions on package. Roll dough very thin with rolling pin. Cover with transparent plastic wrap, tucking edges under pastry to keep airtight.
4. Place saucepan over medium to high heat. Bring to a boil; lower to slow boil. Stir occasionally to keep from sticking. Add more water if necessary. When fruit is tender, measure and stir in sugar, cinnamon, nutmeg and salt. Cook fruit until soft.
5. Drain fruit and then mash through strainer with a fork. (You may need adult help.)
6. Preheat oven to 400°F.
7. Remove wrap from dough and cut into 4-inch rounds with biscuit cutter or jar lid.
8. Place 1 teaspoon in center of each round. Moisten edges of pastry rounds lightly with water. Fold over and press edges together with fork.
9. Place on cookie sheet. Using pot holders, put into oven and bake 12 to 14 minutes until golden. Remove to rack and cool.

Makes about 20 to 24 rounds.

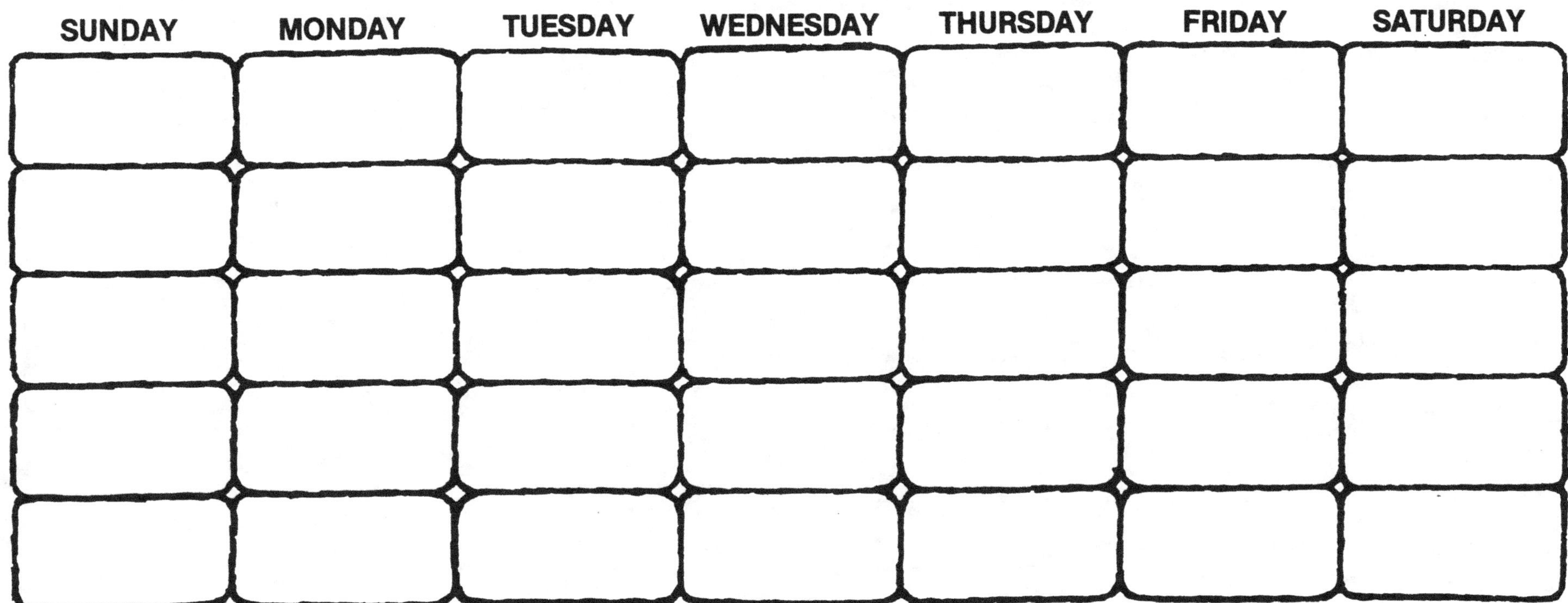